FERN HOUSE

FERN HOUSE

A Year in an Artist's Garden

BY DEBORAH SCHENCK

TEXT BY LAURI BERKENKAMP

CHRONICLE BOOKS

SAN FRANCISCO

Library of Congress Cataloging-in-Publication Data:

Schenck, Deborah.
    Fern House : year in an artist's garden / by Deborah Schenck ;
        text by Lauri Berkenkamp. p. cm.
    ISBN 0-8118-2835-2
        1. Gardening—Vermont—Anecdotes. 2. Gardeners—Vermont—Anecdotes.
        3. Artists—Vermont—Anecdotes. 4. Schenck, Deborah—Homes and haunts—
        Vermont. I. Berkenkamp, Lauri. II. Title.

SB455 .S34 2001
635'.0974—dc21

Printed in Hong Kong

Designed by Edith S. Crocker

Distributed in Canada by Raincoast Books
9050 Shaughnessy Street
Vancouver, British Columbia V6P 6E5

10 9 8 7 6 5 4 3 2 1

Chronicle Books LLC
85 Second Street
San Francisco, California 94105

www.chroniclebooks.com

This book is dedicated to my husband, James,
and my children, Olivia and Daniel.
It is also especially dedicated
to my mother, Sally Hallowell-Carew,
and all mothers learning to balance
the joys of motherhood and their passions in life.

Table of Contents

Fern House: My Own Country Garden

I have always wanted a garden of my own. I grew up in England, a place of rose gardens and country lanes, where green meadows and rolling hills are carpeted in spring with wildflowers. When I left England for America, I promised myself that wherever I lived, I would create a garden for myself like those I had left behind, one that is as reflective and full of detail as the artwork I create.

My husband, James, and I found just such a place in Fern House, a stately brick federal surrounded by woods and sunny fields in a tiny town in Vermont. Built in 1820 and owned by Reuben Morey, a prominent early Vermonter for whom one of the state's many lakes is named, the house sits at the crest of a steep hill and welcomes all who make the journey up from the town green far below. As its name implies, Fern House is surrounded with lush ferns of all kinds, softening the contours of the house with a fine, green filigree. Fern House is warm, comfortable, and welcoming, and I knew as soon as I saw it that it was the place I had been searching for—a place to raise our small daughter, Olivia, and coming baby, and to put down our own roots and become part of a close-knit community.

This book is devoted to the first year I have spent creating my garden, and to the beauty I have found there. My artwork celebrates the importance of the single image—the portrait that holds all the perfume, color and detail of the garden in one perfect bloom. They are quiet images, and they invite people to slow down, to focus and contemplate the small but important details of our world that are so often overlooked. I have worked to create a garden that invites visitors to stop and remember the importance and beauty of individual moments in time.

Each part of the garden inspires my art and reflects many moods. The quiet, shady grotto and pond offer a place to muse under a bower of hydrangea. Sunny beds of perennials and annuals brighten the side garden with bursts of color around the tranquil beauty of the rose arch. Hanging baskets decorate the weathered, brick outer walls and formal entrance at the front of the house.

It has been a year since we first arrived at Fern House, a year of great discovery and many lessons—about gardening, and about life. The garden itself taught me not only the careful process of nurturing new plants as they take root and grow, but also how to laugh and learn from my mistakes. The weeds I left and the flowers I weeded out, the patient replanting of all the seedlings that Olivia or the dogs helped to dig up—all have been part of these life lessons. This book is a celebration of this journey of discovery, and of the simple pleasures that gardening—and life—can offer.

Winter

My story begins in the winter of 1999. I sit in front of the window, garden catalogs on my lap, and watch the snow piling up in huge drifts all around the house, a clean white canvas. My gardening project is already underway, and I have drawn plans and made lists of plants I'll need for the months to come. Winter gardening is simple—so few weeds, such a cozy fire.

Today I took my daughter, Olivia, and the dogs for a short walk on the road as the snow fell. I laughed at the three sets of tracks they made in the new snow—Olivia's tiny footprints flanked on either side by Hannah's and Coogan's as they rolled and jumped in the drifts.

Vermont winters are full of contrast. Some days the snow comes blustering in with great sound and fury; on others, like this one, it showers the ground with soft feathers of white. Snowmen stand in yards and meadows along the road, cheerfully guarding buried gardens and snow-covered porches. Cross-country skiers and our neighbor's horse-drawn sleigh leave long tracks in the unplowed road.

Olivia, only two, is impatient with me these days. She can't understand why I'm so slow and tentative outside on the ice when I used to be so much fun outdoors. In another two months the baby will be born.

Not too long from now, I'll smell the smoke from our neighbor's sugarhouse as he boils down sap gathered from his maple trees, and the redwing blackbirds will flit through the hedge, signaling the end of winter. When the snow melts for good, and snowmen and sleigh rides are simply good memories of our first winter here at Fern House, I'll look back on these quiet indoor months and laugh at myself, I'm sure, remembering how impatient I was for changes to come.

I love our new home and the stark beauty of Vermont winters—
trees and hills, snow-covered roofs and rocky ledges are transformed
into a patchwork of white, heathered greens, grays, and purples.
They are quiet colors, so unlike the bright palette
of summer, but they suit this time of year,
when people stay indoors, and night comes so early.

After the snowstorm this morning,
the house and world outside is strangely quiet—
the snow absorbs sound and dampens every noise.
It smoothes and softens the contours of the land
until nothing looks familiar except the fence surrounding the garden.
As the skies clear, the new snow sparkles
like handfuls of diamonds in the sunshine.

The maples that line our garden remind me of old women dancing.
They bow and sway and whisper to the paper birches
that flank them as the wind blows through their bare branches.

The sun shone so warmly today that I ventured out for a walk with a friend.
We passed an old yellow birch, its silvery bark curling off the trunk in feathery ruffles.
She showed me a Vermont secret, she broke a twig off a sapling,
and it smelled of the fresh mint of early spring.

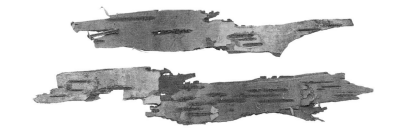

Maple Sugaring

The nights are still very cold,
but the days dawn sunny and grow warmer.
Warm days and cold nights
make the sap flow from the maple trees.

All over Vermont, locals hang metal buckets
from maple trees lining roads, high on hillsides, and
scattered in backyards, waiting for the first sap run.
Soon the sweet, smoky smell of boiling sap will rise
from sugarhouses in every valley and hollow.
Sugaring time has begun.

A pair of blue jays swooped down into the apple trees today,
their feathers flashing bright blue in the sun as they settled briefly
on the birdbath, heralding spring and warmer weather.

Spring

It is finally spring, although for a long time I had trouble seeing how spring in Vermont differs from winter. My son, Daniel, was born in late March, bringing new life and great joy to our house. Outdoors, though, the garden seemed to awaken painfully slowly. I have found myself comparing spring in Vermont to spring in England, and I shouldn't—where there are snowdrops and bluebells covering the newly green ground in England, here there is mud, miles and miles of mud.

Spring in Vermont is signaled by Town Meeting Day on the first Tuesday of March, a day when people in the small towns scattered throughout the state come together to discuss their town's needs, to vote on spending tax dollars and to shake off the chill and isolation of a long winter. Town Meeting heralds the end of winter and the start of a new season, regardless of how much snow is left on the ground, or how much mud is yet to come, sucking our boots off our feet or leaving dirty swaths across kitchen floors.

Spring bulbs, first the crocus and snow drops, then daffodil, and finally tulips, have emerged from their long winter dormancy. It's wonderful to see the garden greening up after such a long time, but now I can see where I have my work cut out for me. The bulbs are lovely, but there are large patches of the garden that need to be filled with annuals and herbs. I have been planting like crazy, taking advantage of the warming days and frost-free nights. Most of my perennials went in last fall when they were big enough to split and much less expensive to buy.

Creating a garden is very different from photographing one—I try to stress the simplicity of images, but my garden, even now in its early stages, is already full of happy mayhem. I don't know for sure what I'm doing, but the garden is growing, the days are sunny, and spring is here!

Friends and family have filled the house with freesias, my favorite flower,
to celebrate Daniel's birth. Their sweet, airy scent will forever remind me of the birth
of my son, and of the wonderful generosity and welcome I have been given here.

Freesia

Originally from South Africa, freesias grow from corms into single-
or double-flowering blooms. Because they are very temperature sensitive,
freesias do not perennialize well, and prefer mild climates.
They bloom in shades of white, yellow, cream, blue, red, pink, lavender,
and orange, and are most often used as a cut flower,
especially during winter months.

The snow is gone from all but the shadiest areas of the garden,
and the vivid green tips of early blooming bulbs are poking through the soil.
The snowdrops and crocus have already pushed their way
through the last patches of snow and brighten
the dark ground with splashes of soft purple, white, and yellow.

The daffodil bulbs I planted last fall
have come up at last and are blooming with
riotous yellow abandon in all parts of the
garden in bunches of twos and threes.
I look at their bright bells nodding
in the sun and wish I were a poet.

Spring seems to blossom overnight.
Every morning I wake to find
the world a bit greener than
the day before. The apple trees
are now in full bloom,
their branches all but hidden
under a canopy of pink and white.
When the wind blows,
showers of sweet-smelling petals
drift in the air.

*A gentle
but persistent rain today
filled the tulip cups and made their
red and yellow blooms appear even more vibrant
in a world turned quite gray.*

Tulips

The name "tulip" is derived from
the Latin word for turban—"tulipa."
Tulips were originally mountain plants,
thriving at high elevations.

A walk around newly raked beds confirms small sprouts of perennials
pushing through the earth. I am heady from the smell of the hyacinths,
one of the earliest blooming bulbs. The annuals and herbs sit patiently in their pots
beside my watering can, waiting to take their places in the garden.

Hyacinth

First cultivated by the ancient Greeks and Romans, highly perfumed hyacinths
are natives of Turkey and the Middle East. In the sixteenth century,
Dutch hybridizers created the full, plump variety found in most formal gardens today.
Hyacinths are a symbol of style and elegance—in the eighteenth century, the gardens
of Louis XV's palace at Versailles were filled with hyacinths of all colors.

Pansies

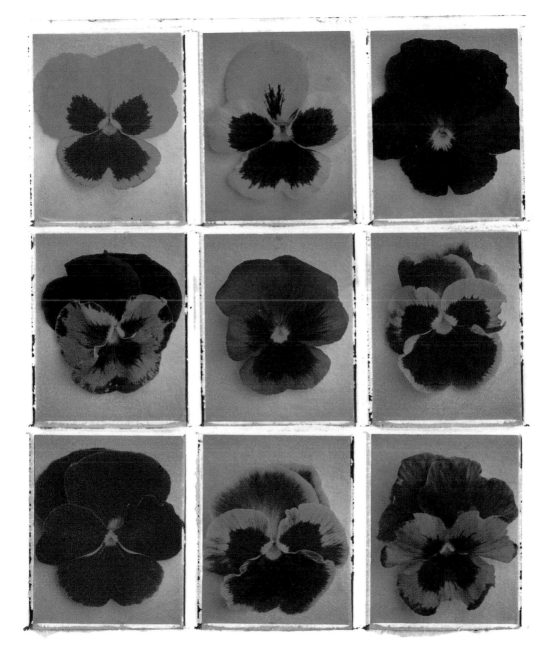

The fiddlehead ferns scattered at the edge of the woods
that contribute to Fern House's name are ready for picking and eating.
Fiddlehead salad is a spring delicacy, as fleeting as the season.

Fiddlehead Salad

Fiddleheads must be cooked to be eaten.
Be sure to buy your fiddleheads from a reliable source,
since some varieties of ferns can be toxic.
Wash the fiddleheads thoroughly and snip off any black ends.
Steam them until they are tender but still crunchy (about 15 minutes).
Remove from heat and plunge into ice water to stop cooking.
Remove from the water and drain.

Fiddleheads can be eaten alone or be tossed with pecans or other sweet nuts
and dressed with vinaigrette for a delicate spring salad.

Trillium

Here and there on my morning walks I see trillium,
one of spring's most beautiful and delicate wildflowers,
peeking through the shady undergrowth.
Trillium first flowers after six years in a stable environment;
once it is established, it blooms every spring thereafter.

Grape Hyacinths

Lily of the Valley

I walked under the tall, arching,
old-fashioned lilacs today,
breathing in the sweet, dusky scent
of the blooms overhead.
Last year a wren
raised a family in the branches,
leaving behind an empty,
fragile-looking nest of wispy grass.
Later I heard chirping
and discovered
a new nest under the porch eaves
filled with anxious chicks
waiting to be fed.

Summer

Vermont summers make up for every minute of our cold, muddy springs. The weather is gorgeous—warm, sunlit days with low humidity, and cool, clear, star-filled nights. Summer lasts only a short time in New England, and everyone—especially gardeners—spend as much time as possible outdoors. Flowers here have adapted to the short growing season and bloom all at once in a profusion of color, making Vermont country gardens both lush and challenging to maintain.

This summer has proved that gardening isn't a pastime for the easily discouraged. The hanging baskets I planted along the brick front of the house haven't grown as they should; instead of a cascade of flowers, they hold dead, soggy stumps. I had put newspaper in the bottom of the planters to save on soil, and the wet paper stopped up all the drainage holes, drowning the seedlings. I have had to start all over, and learned a good lesson about the poor value of day-old news.

The weeds have found the garden a healthy and happy place to make a home—like my new son Daniel, they seem to grow overnight. It's easy to let the whole garden go for a day or two at a time, though, to enjoy the glorious Vermont summer—swims at the town pond, long walks, picnics and lots of berry picking. Wild raspberry and blackberry bushes grow at the edges of the lanes and old meadows all over Vermont. We walk and pick berries as we go, gathering bowlfuls to enjoy with Vermont's famous ice cream.

On summer evenings the air is soft and warm, and swallows swoop and dive through the air long into sunset, hunting for insects. At night fireflies flash by like miniature fireworks displays in the blackness, and the songs of peepers and crickets join with the splashing sounds of the brook, making a lovely racket. I often sit by the pond in the twinkling darkness and wish summer would last forever.

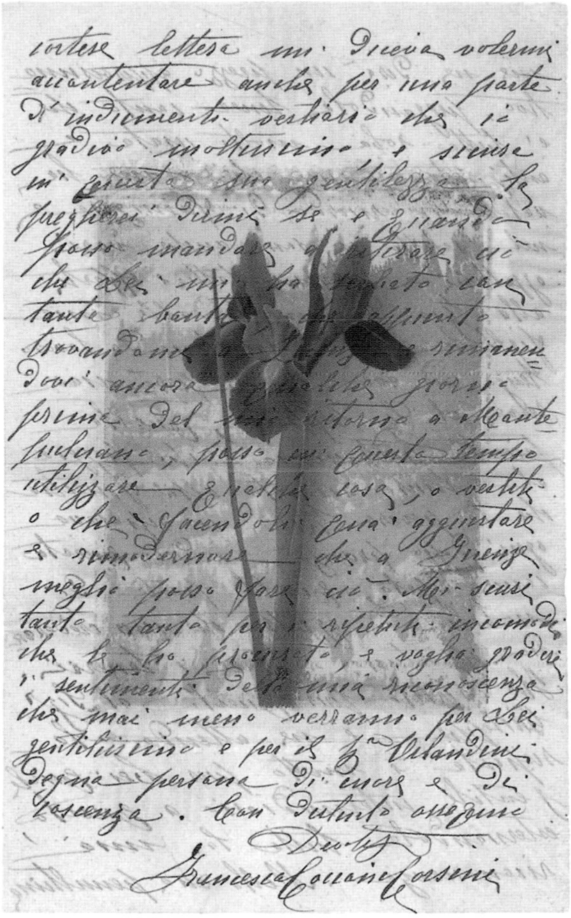

Iris

The bleeding hearts have emerged, vibrant and strong, after a long winter.
Here and there columbine gracefully creep up alongside the old brick walls of the house.

The rhododendrons at the bottom of the garden are a favorite place for butterflies.
Their gentle colors and protected location attract butterflies of all kinds.

Every day brings unexpected surprises.
This morning I turned a corner and discovered a carpet of blue—
periwinkle, forget-me-not, and violets peeking through the leaves.
At the next turn I was overwhelmed with red.

Coneflower

Primula

Dahlia

Bee Balm

Roses

Roses can be difficult to grow in Vermont, since the frost reaches so deeply
into the ground during the long winters. The blooms on roses that grow here
are often smaller than roses grown in warmer places, the color more vivid,
a reflection of the short, but intense growing season here in the north country.

We came back from a two-week holiday to find every bed completely
overgrown with weeds. Vetch, its curly tendrils snaking around
everything, is a beautiful, but formidable intruder.
Daunting hours of meticulous weeding lie ahead,
pulling each clinging vine from around the other plants.
I will never get the dirt out
from under my fingernails . . .

Ferns

Bracken
Chain Fern
Fancy Fern
Glade Fern
Horsetail Fern
Lace-leaf Fern
Lady Fern
Maidenhair Fern
Mountain Wood Fern
Ostrich Fern
Vermont Wood Fern

I have tried to count the varieties   of ferns that flourish here —
some lacy, some feathery,   some as sharp as saw teeth —
but there are so many   I have decided instead
to simply enjoy their   subtle differences
and their wonderful addition to the landscape.

Nasturtiums are delicious
in my summer salads.
The bright, peppery blossoms,
and cresslike leaves
make the simplest lunch seem exotic.

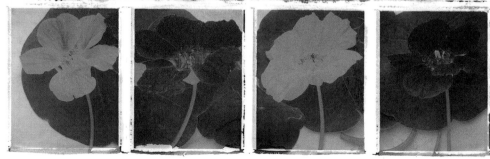

Evening Primrose

Bellflower

Loosestrife

Gentian

Geranium

Harebell

Lilies

Hydrangea

The Pond

The weedy, boggy area below the wildflower meadow
has been transformed into a lovely, rock-lined water
garden and pond. We bought one hundred goldfish
and watched our children introduce them to their
new home. It seems as if every frog in the
neighborhood has staked out territory around the
bullrushes. Late in the day we hung up the hammock between
two nearby trees, and listened to the sound of the water spilling
over the rocks in a quiet celebration.

Cattails

Wildflowers

I sent Olivia out to the meadow to pick wildflowers for the table.

She waded through the flowers, sending them swaying in her wake.

Her favorites are the vividly colored cosmos in shades of bright pink, white, and fuschia.

She brought in enough blossoms to fill all the milk bottles I could find.

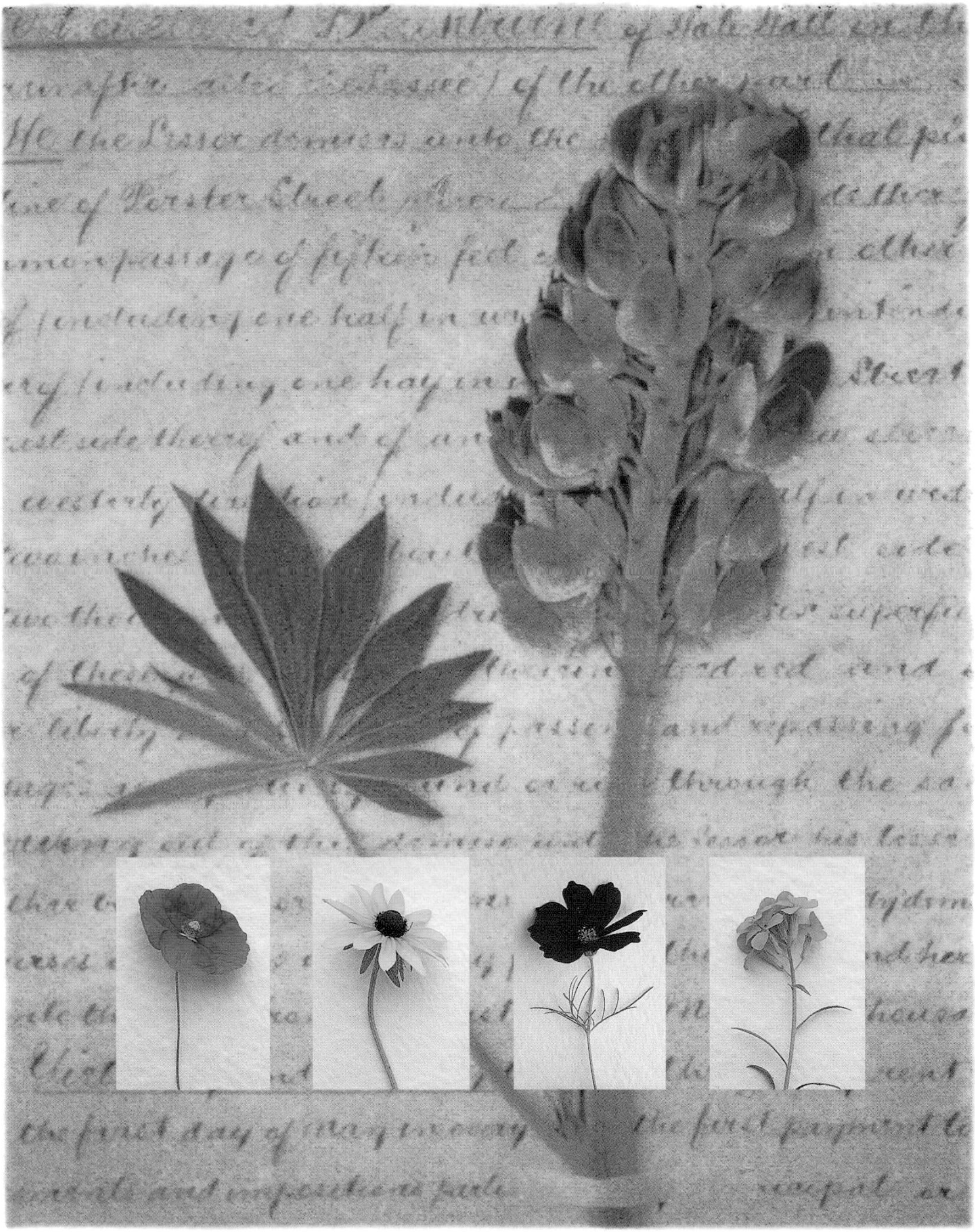

Pontentilla

Trout Lily

Cowparsnip

Buttercup

Pontentilla

Cowparsnip

Buttercups have sprung up
all over the garden,
even where they aren't especially welcome.
I should pull them, but I can't —
they remind me of when I was a child
and held them under my chin,
their pale yellow glow against my skin
that tell-tale sign of liking butter.

Poppies

So many scarlet heads in motion wave,
moving together with a ripple strength
of gentle oceans, on a summer day.
—Sally Hallowell-Carew

*Red clover is the state flower of Vermont—
and like the people who live here, it has a
simple beauty and surprising, unexpected
sweetness. In summer, pastures are
transformed into carpets of soft, pinky red.*

Berry Jam

This recipe works well
for any seeded berry.

·

4 cups berries
3 cups sugar

·

Wash fruit thoroughly
and remove stems,
leaves, or any other debris.
Put the berries in a large pot
and crush them.
Cook for 15 minutes
to reduce the juices.
Add the sugar
and bring to a boil.
Cook, stirring,
until the sugar dissolves.
Boil rapidly until the mixture
reaches jelling point
on a candy thermometer.
Skim off the foam
and let stand until cool.
Pour into sterilized
jam jars and seal.
Makes approximately
2 pints of jam.

Berry picking is a favorite summer excursion.
Berries, both cultivated and wild,
grow in profusion throughout Vermont,
some in neat, well-tended beds,
and others hanging from brambles
and peeking from under leaves by roadsides.
Olivia and I spend hours each summer
picking strawberries and raspberries
at local farms and making jam
to give to family and friends.

Daisies and black-eyed susans are happy travelers, popping up everywhere where there is lots of sun. Originally prairie flowers, they are a cheerful reminder that...

...no matter how carefully I plan my garden,
Mother Nature has her own ideas about where flowers should bloom.

The Herb Garden

The herb garden sits in a
protected spot just outside
the kitchen window, sheltered
by a winding clematis.
Rosemary, tarragon, chives,
mint, and thyme thrive in a bed
that last year held only a
tangle of weeds and old leaves.
I can pop out of the door
and snip chives for salads
on my way to the table.

The chives have bloomed in a spiky burst at the corner of the herb garden.
Their pungent, onion aroma reminds me of the summer garden luncheons of my childhood.

Parsley
Sage
St. John's Wart
Oregano

Lavender
Chives
Lamb's Quarters
Thyme

Rosemary
Tarragon
Chive
Lavender

Basil Sage Lavendar

Oregano Chives Parsley

The Meaning of Herbs

Basil: Passion • Sage: Wisdom • Lavender: Love, Friendship, and Devotion
Oregano: Joy, Happiness • Chives: Cheerfulness • Parsley: Gratitude • Mint: Hospitality
Lemon Balm: Relaxation • Thyme: Activity • Rosemary: Remembrance

I can tell when the dogs
  have been lying in the herb garden —
    they come in the house, tracking dirt
      and smelling of fresh mint.

Mint : Hospitality.

My neighbors over the hill harvested
some of their honey today. Their hives
are full of dripping gold that tastes
of red clover and fresh flowers.
I brought home a piece of honeycomb
full of the taste of summer.

Today Olivia and I found a dead wood thrush lying in the grass.
I gently picked it up to show her its perfect, smooth feathers.
Olivia was full of questions about death and heaven, and together
we buried the thrush in a quiet corner of the grotto.

It's haying time—hot, dry, and windy, the fields tall with grass
ready for the first cutting. Throughout the valley, farmers are on their tractors harvesting,
tedding, and baling hay for the winter, racing against storm clouds on the horizon.
I can hear the thumping of balers echoing up the hill long into twilight.

Corn

Bravado • Double Gem • Hopi Blue Flour
Lancelot • Mandan Bride • Platinum Lady • Quickie
Seneca Appaloosa • Silver Queen • Spring Snow

It has been a good year for sweet corn—hot and dry.
Friends in the village have grown so much that they invited our whole town
to a corn boil. They served up fresh ears of corn dripping in butter
to all who passed by. It was a lovely way to celebrate late summer.

The Farmer's Market

From May to October, local farmers gather once a week to sell fruits and vegetables, cheese and flowers, all arranged in bright stacks. Barefoot children race by, laughing and playing, as people browse at the stalls and pile their baskets high with fresh produce. The tangy, earthy smell of garden vegetables permeates the air.

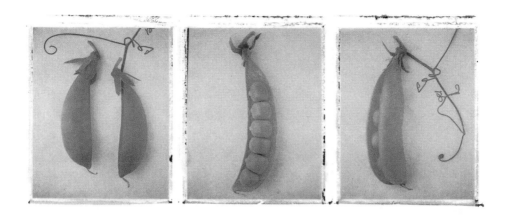

I stopped at a stall and chose peas and beans from a basket, their tendrils still curling delicately around the pods. The sugar snap peas are an early summer treat here, so sweet and delicious that one can eat them, pod and all, straight from the vine.

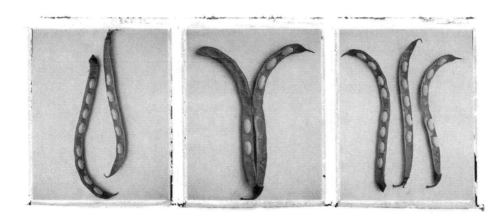

At the farmer's
market I met
a tiny boy
sitting with a jar
filled with sunflowers
taller than he was.
I bought all
of his sunflowers
and a kiss.
Money well spent.

Autumn We had a frost last night! This morning I walked outside to get the paper and my footprints cut a path through grass covered in a soft, white coat. It melted as soon as the sun rose higher, but frost is the first sign that fall has arrived.

Autumn is my favorite time of the year for many reasons; it's the light that appeals to me the most, as it filters through the changing foliage, burnishing everything with a soft, yellow glow. As a family we turn to the rituals that characterize the change in seasons—together we bring out woolly sweaters from chests, put comforters and flannel sheets on beds and wake up to frost-etched windows.

Fall in our part of Vermont is also marked by the return of the country fair. Each September for more than a century the old fairgrounds in the town over the hill transforms for a week into a loud and gaudy midway filled with livestock competitions, pig races, demolition derbies, produce and craft competitions, rides, games, and terrible food. This year in the children's competition, we entered some of the hardy asters Olivia helped to plant and she won a white ribbon. I have grand plans for her horticultural future.

We have put the gardens to bed with a feeling just short of regret—I'm ready to spend less time gardening for now, but I have so enjoyed this summer that it's hard for me to let it go. We cut down the dead heads of all the spent perennials and mulched the beds with composted manure and mulch hay for insulation against the cold. I will plant a few new perennials—day lilies, rudbeckia, hosta, or whatever is on sale at the nursery—in the next several days, then I'll officially end my first year in the garden at Fern House.

I have enjoyed every moment.

The crabapples are red,
ripe, and heavy
on their branches.
They are one of the first
fall fruits to ripen,
and make delicious
amber-colored jam.

Sweet, tart blackberries
nestled between sharp thorns
offer a pleasurable treat
to those who pick carefully.
When they are gone,
it's a sign that autumn
is officially here.

Foliage season is reaching its peak—
the hillsides are afire with color. The red
maples are the first hardwoods to change
color; the leaves flash bright crimson as
early as the beginning of September, while
the rest of the trees remain summer green. Their
leaves will change from green to red, orange, yellow,
and every shade and mixture in between. The last trees
to turn are the tamaracks—their drooping needles fade to yellow
before dropping off and signaling the end of fall.

Apples

Blushing Golden
Braeburn
Cortland
Empire
Gala
Ginger Gold
Golden Delicious
Gravenstein
Idared
Jonagold
McIntosh
Macoun
Northern Spy
Red Delicious
Red Rome
Rhode Island Greening
Russet
Spartan
Spigold
Yellow Newtown

*My neighbor brought over apples from the final
harvest of the year. Soon we'll join friends in the
autumn ritual of cider pressing, taking turns
cranking the heavy handle of the antique press
as it crushes the apples until clear, sweet-tart juice
runs out into the oak bucket below,
attracting bees and curious children.*

Pumpkins

Autumn Gold
Baby Pam
Big Max
Connecticut Field
Howden
Jack Be Little
Lady Godiva
Long Island Cheese
Long Pie
Lumina
New England Pie
Rouge Vif d'Etampes
Wee-B-Little
Young's Beauty

❧

At Halloween all the children in town
bring carved pumpkins
to place on the steps of the town hall.
At dusk, the glowing jack-o-lanterns
preside over a town-wide costume parade.

The thistle is the last flower to bloom.   My mother once told me that thistles
are a symbol of hearth and home, their prickly, protective outer leaves
are like the brick and mortar walls of the house, and the delicate, purple blossoms
represent the beauty and warmth of the family within.

Last night's hard frost
has glazed the dog's bowl of water
by the back door.
I have put the garden to bed,
and the season is officially over.

It has been a very special year.

Before and After

The following pages document the before-and-after story of Fern House. Some shots of the garden were taken by previous owners of the house; others show our work on the garden to date. My overall plans for the garden were very ambitious and I soon realized that it will take many years to fulfill the vision I have for my garden. It is truly a "work in progress."

The first and easiest job was to sow the wild-flowers in the meadow above the house. With the help of friends and family members, we quickly had a very rewarding field of color to enjoy.

The hanging baskets  wrap the house in an abundance of flowers. Their cascading color is a gorgeous complement to the bright annuals and soft perennials in the gardens below.

Making the pond was the most dramatic change. We used the foundation of an old barn for its creation. It was a tremendous amount of work removing weeds from the area and digging the necessary pit. We completed the project with a professional pond kit, and to the delight of our young children, one hundred goldfish joined our household. The grotto was an extension of the pond area that we filled with shady plants and mosses—it is a quiet place for reflection with gracious statues and the sound of the waterfall.

Finally, I knew I wanted to create a large, herbaceous border that would mature over the years. The obvious place was the south terrace. Seven-foot weeds were gradually torn out and replaced with perennials, shrub annuals, and small hydrangea trees.

Overall, these endeavors have yielded a great feeling of accomplishment, but there is always more to do!

Before

Preparing the Soil

Sowing the Seeds

The Second Sowing

Rolling the Seeds In

Blooming

Sowing Wildflowers

Wildflowers need very little to thrive in Vermont—a sunny location, bare soil, and adequate moisture. These are the steps to follow for a wildflower garden:

1. Cultivate the soil until it is clear of weeds and grass.
2. Mix wildflower seed with sand so the seed disperses evenly over the ground.
3. Press the scattered seed into the ground lightly— a lawn roller works best.
4. Keep the area moist.

In the spring and summer of the first year after planting, annuals such as cosmos, sunflowers, cornflowers, and poppies will bloom in the wildflower meadow. These annuals usually self-seed each year. In the second year of blooming, and subsequent years thereafter, perennials such as lupine, phlox, daisies, and mallow will bloom and spread throughout the garden.

The Pond

Before

Digging

Foundation

After

The Grotto

Before

After

Hanging Baskets

Hanging baskets are time-consuming but not difficult to make. They can be lined with either sphagnum moss, shade cloth, or black plastic. None of these liners will be seen once the plants start to grow over the sides of the basket. To prepare a hanging basket, follow these steps:

Soak sphagnum moss in a bucket of water for one hour. Squeeze most of the water out, and place handfuls of moss in the bottom of the basket, molding up the sides to about $\frac{1}{3}$ of the basket's height. The moss should be about 1 to 2 inches thick. Fill this with potting mix and wet it down. Place plants for the sides of the basket in rows through the moss so the roots are in the soil, making sure that the plant plugs in each row are not directly above the plugs in the previous row. Continue placing moss up the rest of the basket until it is about $1\frac{1}{2}$ inches above the rim of the basket. Fill with mix just to the top of the basket, not to the top of the moss, and wet it down.

If using shade cloth or black plastic as basket liners, fully line the basket and leave up to 4 inches of extra material over the top of the basket's rim. Clip the extra with clothespins over the rim until planting is finished, then carefully trim the material to within 3 inches of the basket's edge. Be sure to puncture holes in the bottom of the black plastic for drainage. To plant the sides of the basket, cut holes just large enough to push the plug through, making sure the rows of plants are staggered.

Plant upright plants in the center of the basket, with cascading plants out toward the sides. This will create a basket with few gaps and lush blooms. The hanging baskets will need fertilizing with a 20-20-20 combination at least once a week throughout the blooming season.

Herb Garden

Includes: 1. Basil 2. Lavender 3. Sage 4. Chives 5. Lemon Balm 6. Rosemary
7. Thyme 8. Tarragon 9. Johnny-jump-up

Before

After

South Terrace

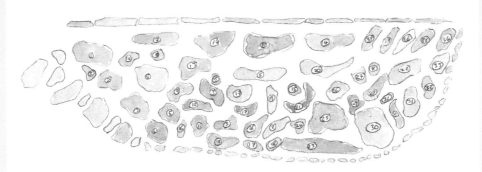

Includes: 1. Baptisia   2. Jacob's Ladder   3. Japanese Primrose   4. Lily of the valley
5. Companula   6. Meadow Rue   7. Globe Flower   8. Hydrangea Tree   9. Columbine
10. Lungwort   11. Ladybells   12. Lady's Mantle   13. Astilbe   14. Delphinium
15. Rhododendron   16. Primula   17. Bleeding Heart   18. Dianthus   19. Peony
20. Joe Pye Weed   21. Yarrow   22. Geranium   23. Catchfly   24. Catnip   25. Coreopsis
26. Pincushion Flower   27. Bachelor Button   28. Vinca   29. Marguarite
30. Poppy   31. Penstemon   32. Limonium   33. Speedwell
34. Hydrangea   35. Bellflower   36. Foxglove   37. Salvia   38. Gayfeather

Before

After

Acknowledgements

I would like to thank the following people for their help and support in creating this book—without them *Fern House* would not have been possible. My husband, James, and my mother for all their hard work. My sister Kate and her husband, Angelo, for making the trellis and sowing wildflowers. My friends, Lauri Berkenkamp for her choice of words and Edie Crocker for her excellent design. Dawn Griffis for her advise on gardening. Jim and Roz Finn and Elizabeth Shealy for the honey and haying. Sheila Paget for the "mother" poem. Charlie Brown for his help with maple sugaring. Eric Thorp for the pond. Tom Gerlach for all his financial wisdom. Denny and May Emerson for their photos of the house. Derby Farms, Edgewater Farm, and Standing Stone Farm for their plants and flowers.

I would also like to thank the following companies for their generous donations of products and services:

Dawn Griffis. Gardening consultant and hanging baskets. 603-353-2123

Foxtail Flowers. Freesia and other flowers. 888-390-6100

Frenchwyres. Wire arch and chair. 903-581-6749

Gardener's Eden. Fairy statue. 800-822-1214

Longacres Nursery. St. Francis and angel statue. 603-448-6110

The Elegant Earth. Stone bench and birdbath. 205-324-6464

The Vermont Wildflower Farm. Wildflowers. 802-425-3500